FOR LAUGHING OUT LOUDER

MORE POEMS TO TICKLE YOUR FUNNYBONE

Selected by Jack Prelutsky
Pictures by Marjorie Priceman

Alfred A. Knopf · New York

To Julia, Susan, Mary and Rick

—J. P.

To my Father

—M. P.

THIS IS A BORZOI BOOK PUBLISHED BY ALFRED A. KNOPF, INC.

Compilation copyright © 1995 by Alfred A. Knopf, Inc.
Illustrations copyright © 1995 by Marjorie Priceman
"I Often Wonder" and "Madame Leopard Reflects" copyright
© 1995 by Jack Prelutsky

Library of Congress Cataloging-in-Publication Data
For laughing out louder: more poems to tickle your funnybone /
selected by Jack Prelutsky; illustrated by Marjorie Priceman.
p.   cm.
Summary: A collection of humorous poems by a variety of authors
including John Ciardi, X. J. Kennedy, Eve Merriam, and William Jay Smith.
ISBN 0-679-87063-6 (trade)
ISBN 0-679-97063-0 (lib. bdg.)
1. Humorous poetry, American. 2. Children's poetry, American.
[1. American poetry—Collections. 2. Humorous poetry.]
I. Prelutsky, Jack. II. Priceman, Marjorie, ill. PS 595.H8F69 1995
811'.07089282—dc20 94-40655

Manufactured in the United States of America 10 9 8 7 6 5 4 3 2 1

Acknowledgments of permission to reprint previously published material
can be found at the back of the book.

Contagious

Shut the windows,
Lock the locks,
Gretchen's got the chicken socks.

So contagious,
It's outrageous,
She's really got the blues.
I guess we should be glad
She didn't catch the chicken shoes.

—Brod Bagert

There Seems to Be a Problem

I really don't know about Jim.
When he comes to our farm for a swim,
    The fish, as a rule,
    Jump out of the pool.
Is there something the matter with him?

–John Ciardi

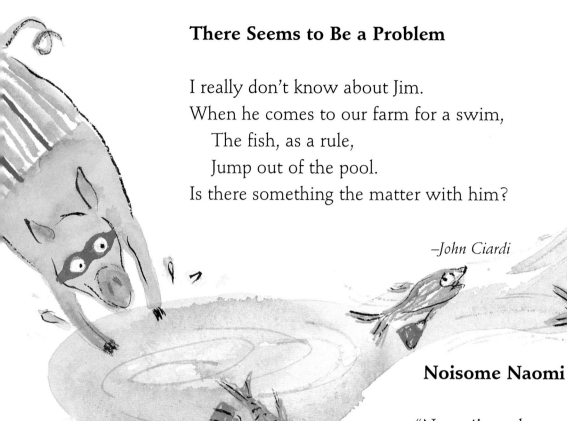

Noisome Naomi

"Naomi's such a nuisance,"
  The neighbors all complain.
"That nasty little numbskull,
  She's at it once again.

"Her voice is like a needle,
  Her tales are never true.
  Her language is so noxious
  It turns the devil blue!

"Naomi is a nightmare,
  She's nervy as a newt.
  Her ma and pa are nitwits—
  They think Naomi's cute."

–Jeanne Steig

Toes in My Nose

I stuck my toes
In my nose
And I couldn't get them out.
It looked a little strange
And people began to shout,
"Why would you ever?
My goodness—I never!"
They got in a terrible snit.
It's simple, I said
As they put me to bed,
I just wanted to see
If they fit.

—Sheree Fitch

A Young Lady Named Rose

There was a young lady named Rose
Who was constantly blowing her nose;
    Because of this failing
    They sent her off whaling
So the whalers could say: "Thar she blows!"

—William Jay Smith

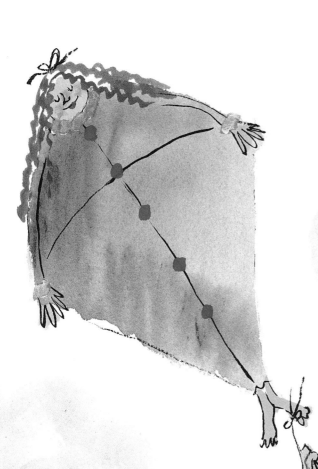

My Sister

My sister's remarkably light,
She can float to a fabulous height.
It's a troublesome thing,
But we tie her with string,
And we use her instead of a kite.

–*Margaret Mahy*

The Human Beanpole

The thinnest man I ever saw
Was called "The Human Beanpole."
He'd never open any door,
But slip in through the keyhole!

–*Colin McNaughton*

Sir Samuel Squinn

Sir Samuel Squinn,
Sir Samuel Squinn
is very tall
and very thin.
He wears a beard
and—this is weird—
he has no skin!
It's none of our business,
Sir Samuel Squinn,
but how do you keep
your insides in?

–Florence Parry Heide

Big Bert

Big Bert sat on a cushion.
"I'm much too fat," moaned he.
"Who else could be so miserable?"
The cushion answered: "Me!"

–Richard Edwards

7

Madame Leopard Reflects

I'm the loveliest leopard
Beneath the blue sky,
There's no other leopard
As lovely as I.
I'm not only lovely,
I'm sweet as can be—
I'll have you for dinner
If you disagree.

—Wolvar Sprod

A Stripeless Tiger

A stripeless tiger
That's an elephant's size,
With an elephant's trunk
And an elephant's eyes,
That tries to roar
But somehow can't—
Most probably is
Just an elephant.

—Arnold Spilka

The Elephant

Of all the facts about mammals
This is most relevant:
It takes a lot of paper
To gift-wrap an elephant.

–Louis Phillips

Tom Tigercat

Tom Tigercat is noted
for his manners and his wit.
He wouldn't think of lion,
no, he doesn't cheetah bit.
Tom never has pretended
to be something that he's not.
I guess that's why we like him
and why he likes ocelot.

–J. Patrick Lewis

Pangolin

This disrespectful pangolin
Reclines upon a pillow,
And plays upon a mandolin
Made from an armadillo.

To sing his songs is his intent,
At nineteen to the dozen,
And so he strums an instrument
That used to be his cousin.

–Colin West

"Tell Me I'm Pretty," the Bunny Said

"Tell me I'm pretty," the Bunny said,
"Prettier than any other;
 To the Easter parade all bonneted
 I'm going with my mother."

"You are quite pretty," the Ostrich said,
"Prettier than any other;
 But the hat that's sitting upon your head
 Is my dear departed brother."

–Ellen Raskin

Ptarmigans

Ptarmigans should not be pteased
When met upon the ptrail.
For ptarmigans, if pteased, may pturn
And ptweak you in the ptail.

–Pike Johnson, Jr.

Down in Patagonia

Down in Patagonia
A walrus caught pneumonia,
From playing its trombonia
While swimming all alonia.

(So when in Patagonia
A walrus on its ownia
Should play the xylophonia,
To guard against pneumonia.)

–Dennis Lee

11

In Her Lunchbox

In her lunchbox Lena packs
Ornamental fruit of wax,
Adds live worms, a special feature
For her apple for the teacher.

–X. J. Kennedy

Show and Tell

Billy brought his snake to school
For show and tell today.
"This snake belongs to me," he said.
"It's gentle as can be," he said.
"It wouldn't hurt a flea," he said.
But it swallowed him anyway.

–David L. Harrison

12

Brain Drain

The dinosaurs did not remain
Because they had a tiny brain.
But recently, our teacher found
That tiny brains are still around…

—Max Fatchen

Bad Report—Good Manners

My daddy said, "My son, my son,
This school report is bad."
I said, "I did my best I did,
My dad, my dad, my dad."
"Explain, my son, my son," he said,
"Why *bottom* of the class?"
"I stood aside, my dad, my dad,
To let the others pass."

—Spike Milligan

The Trouble with My House

I haven't any windows
And I haven't any doors,
I haven't any ceilings
And I haven't any floors,
I haven't got an attic
And I haven't any halls,
I haven't got a basement
And I haven't any walls,
I haven't got a roof
And that's the reason, I suppose,
Why rain keeps pouring on my head
And dripping off my nose.

–David L. Harrison

Although He Didn't Like the Taste

Although he didn't like the taste,
George brushed his teeth with pickle paste.
Not ever was his mouth so clean,
Not ever were his teeth so green.

–Arnold Lobel

14

Hullo, Inside

Physical-education slides
Show us shots of our insides.
Every day I pat my skin,
"Thanks for keeping it all in."

–Max Fatchen

Insides

I'm very grateful to my skin
For keeping all my insides in—
I do so hate to think about
What I would look like inside-out.

–Colin West

15

Gorilla

Big gorilla
Hairy gorilla
Gorilla looking sad,
The short one with the belly
Reminds me of my dad.

–Brod Bagert

Ancient Egyptian Joke

Father's wrapped in bandages:
Head, arms, legs, and tummy.
Perhaps an explanation's due—
My daddy is a mummy!

–Colin McNaughton

I Often Wonder

I often wonder why I wear
Assorted seafood in my hair,
When I could beautify my bean
With lemons and a tangerine.

—Wolvar Sprod

Oh, How Strange

Oh, how strange is my Uncle Ned!
He wears a cat on his balding head.
When asked why he wears a cat for a wig,
He says that he sneezes when wearing a pig.

—Paul Duggan

Oh, Ozzie!

"Polar bear in the garden!" yelled Ozzie
 And we all rushed out to see,
 But of course it wasn't a bear at all—
 Just a marmalade cat who'd jumped over the wall.
 Oh, Ozzie!

"Mountain lion in the garden!" yelled Ozzie,
 And we all rushed out to see,
 But of course it wasn't a lion with a roar—
 Just the scruffy black dog who'd dug in from next door.
 Oh, Ozzie!

"Kangaroo in the garden!" yelled Ozzie,
 And we all stayed in and smiled,
 And of course it wasn't a kangaroo—
 But a man-eating tiger escaped from the zoo.
 Poor Ozzie.

–Richard Edwards

The Crocodile's Dentist

Here is his mirror, here is his drill,
Here is his briefcase, here is his bill,
Here are his boots on the riverbank, so
Where did the crocodile's dentist go?

–Richard Edwards

The Crocodile—

This is a Crocodile, my boy...
Or is it an Alligator?...
I've an excellent book that you'll enjoy
We can refer to later;

The Alligator...no, Crocodile
Is a purplish color beneath.
Give it a tickle to make it smile
And let's count the number of teeth,

For the Croc. (I think) has a row too few
Though the 'Gator can't wink its eye...

Ah!
      Now I can tell you which of the two
You have just been eaten by.

–Michael Flanders

The Nose Knows

Skunk doesn't smell
exactly like a rose.

One the nose yeses,
one the nose noes.

–Eve Merriam

Elephant Rules

Never be silly or mean
To an elephant,
Never feed chili or beans
To an elephant,
Never go near
To the front or the rear
Of a chilifull, bellyfull
Smellyphant.

–David L. Harrison

Shock Sock

You should have seen the look on my face
When I took off my sock and it flew into space.
A smelly sock packs so much power.
It got to Mars in half an hour.

–Bill Condon

When You Get Old

When you get old
And think you're sweet
Pull off your shoes
And smell your feet.

–Anonymous

Hippopotamus

How far from human beauty
Is the hairless hippopotamus
With such a square enormous head
And such a heavy botamus.

–Mary Ann Hoberman

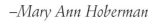

A Hippopotamusn't

A hippopotamusn't sit
   On lawn chairs, stools, and rockers.
A hippopotamusn't yawn
   Directly under tightrope walkers.
A hippopotamusn't roll
   In gutters used by bowlers.
A hippopotamusn't fail
   To floss his hippopotamolars.

The awful things a hippopotamusn't do
Are just
As important as the lawful things
A hippopotamust.

–J. Patrick Lewis

22

Hula Eel

Take an eel,
Make a loop,
Use him as a Hula Hoop.
Feel him twist and twirl and spin,
Down your ankles, round your chin,
Tighter, tighter, tighter yet,
Ain't an eel a lovely pet?
Hey—answer when I talk to you—
Don't just stand there turning blue.

–Shel Silverstein

The Hippopotanoose

Oh, what is fat and comes in coils
Prepared for cowboy use?
The newest thing in lariats:
The Hippopotanoose.

Its only drawback is its size,
For hang it on your saddle
And any normal quarterhorse
Will be inclined to waddle.

But throw it round a running steer,
Or round a big stampede,
The Hippopotanoose will fill
A cowpoke's every need.

–Jane Yolen

The Eel

I don't mind eels
Except as meals.
And the way they feels.

–Ogden Nash

23

I Left My Head

I left my head
somewhere
today.
Put it down for
just
a minute.
Under the
table?
On a chair?
Wish I were
able
to say
where.
Everything I need
is
in it!

–Lilian Moore

Wake Up Early

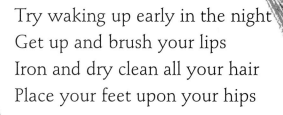

Try waking up early in the night
Get up and brush your lips
Iron and dry clean all your hair
Place your feet upon your hips

Stand up straight while bending down
Stoop to touch the ceiling
Or run away while standing still
It's a quite unusual feeling

Stand up then quick! grab your lap
Before it disappears
Then kiss yourself upon the forehead
Or try to join your ears

If you tried to do these silly things
Before you even tested them
Then you are just as weird
As the person who suggested them.

–Dick Gautier

For Neatness and Comfort

"For neatness and comfort,"
  my grandfather said,
"Take off your boots
  when you stand on your head."

"But," said Aunt Jane,
"does the boy understand
  he should get a receipt
  when he lends them a hand?"

"And have you implored him,"
  inquired Aunt Sue,
"not to use toenails
  where thumbtacks would do?"

"I have simply advised him,"
  my grandfather said,
"to hold on to his hat
  when he's losing his head."

–N. M. Bodecker

It Makes No Difference to Me

I climbed a mountain three feet high
And banged my head against the sky.

"Watch out!" my sister's brother said.
"You climb that high, you'll lose your head!"

I didn't care. Mine is no use
To anyone. What's your excuse?

–John Ciardi

Joker

There's a flicker of a snicker
before Joe tells a joke,
there's a twitter of a titter,
a smiley wily poke,

a trickle of a tee-hee,
a huff of a guffaw,
a snippet of a giggle-snort,
a half of a hee-haw,

a chortle, a chuckle,
a gargantuan grin,
a hoo-hoo-hoo *Ha* HA!
and then he'll begin.

–*Eve Merriam*

Hi, How Are You Today?

I'm feeling very horrible
And low and mean and mad
And dreadful and deplorable
And rotten, sick, and sad
And nasty and unbearable
And hateful, vile, and blue
But thanks a lot for asking
And please tell me…
How are you?

–*Jeff Moss*

26

The Fossilot

You cannot find a Fossilot
Except in ancient stones,
Where imprints of its teeth and claws
Lie jumbled with its bones.

Some scientists cleaned up the bones,
Arranged, then tried to date them.
But when they had the jaw complete—
It turned around and ate them.

–Jane Yolen

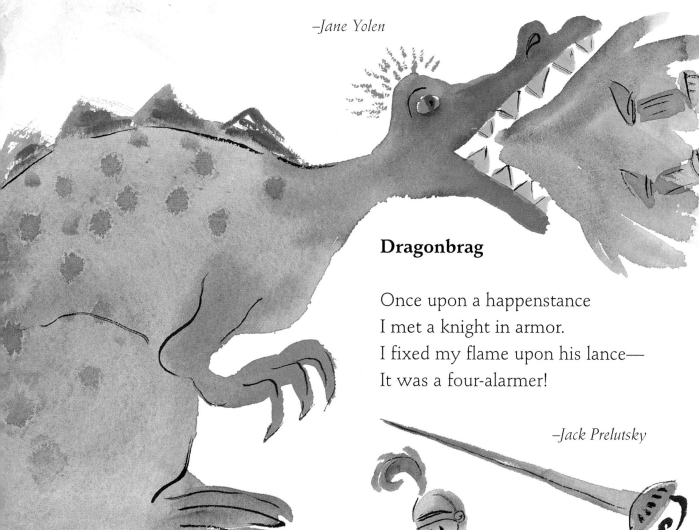

Dragonbrag

Once upon a happenstance
I met a knight in armor.
I fixed my flame upon his lance—
It was a four-alarmer!

–Jack Prelutsky

A Close-Knit Family

Bip and Beep were silly sheep
Who quite upset their mother.
The moment that her back was turned
They tried to knit each other.

—Bill Condon

Birdseed

It didn't work.
I planted birdseed in the ground
And wild weeds sprouted all around.
I know it sounds a bit absurd
But I couldn't grow a single bird.

—Brod Bagert

Harriet, by Magic Force

Harriet, by magic force,
turned herself into a horse.
Combed her pretty ponytail,
ate her dinner from a pail,
snorted water from a trough,
and never took her horseshoes off.

–Eve Merriam

A Better Mousetrap

If you build a better mousetrap
And put it in your house,
Before long, Mother Nature's
Going to build a better mouse.

–Anonymous

Groan!

The baker's making bread,
His brow is hot and beaded,
The pummeled dough
Is happy, though—
It's so nice to be kneaded.

–Richard Edwards

On a Factory Tour

On a factory tour, Will Gossage,
Watching folks make bratwurst sausage,
Jumped into the meat feet-first.

Brats are bad, but Will's the wurst.

–X. J. Kennedy

We're Fearless Flying Hotdogs

We're fearless flying hotdogs,
the famous "Unflappable Five,"
we're mustered in formation
to climb, to dip, to dive,
we spread our wings with relish,
then reach for altitude,
we're aerobatic wieners,
the fastest flying food.

We're fearless flying hotdogs,
we race with flair and style,
then catch up with each other
and soar in single file,
you never saw such daring,
such power and control,
as when we swoop and spiral,
then slide into a roll.

The throngs applaud our antics,
they cheer us long and loud,
there's never a chilly reception,
there's never a sour crowd,
and if we may speak frankly,
we are a thrilling sight,
we're fearless flying hotdogs,
the delicate essence of flight.

–Jack Prelutsky

Homemade Boat

This boat that we just built is just fine—
And don't try to tell us it's not.
The sides and the back are divine—
It's the bottom I guess we forgot....

–Shel Silverstein

New Bicycle

Sunday I got a brand-new bike;
Monday I learned how to ride;
Tuesday I went by my grandmother's house,
And to the countryside.
Wednesday I pedaled up a hill;
Thursday I reached the top;
I'll be home Friday or Saturday—
Or as soon as I learn how to stop.

–Yolanda Nave

Betty Bopper

This is Little Betty Bopper.
She has popcorn in the popper.
Seven pounds of it! Please stop her.
That's more popcorn than is proper
In a popper. Someone drop her
Just a hint! Mommer! Popper!
Betty's going to come a cropper!
Look, it's starting! Get a chopper.
Chop the door down!
 …Well, too late.

–John Ciardi

The Vacuum Cleaner's Swallowed Will

The vacuum cleaner's swallowed Will.
 He's vanished. What a drag!
Still, we can do without him till
 It's time to change the bag.

–X. J. Kennedy

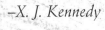

Skeletons in Restaurants

Skeletons in restaurants
Should wear enormous bibs
To catch the peas and other things
That don't stick to their ribs.

–Paul Duggan

Bomb Appetit!

"If you eat one more slice of pie,
    Then you will burst, I fear."

"Oh, that's a risk I'll gladly take.
    But just in case—stand clear!"

–Colin McNaughton

Shake-'n'-Bake a Jelly

If you want a jelly dinner
That's as tasty as can be,
You can shake-'n'-bake a jelly
With a special recipe.

First you bake it in the oven
In a jelly-baking pan;
Then you plop it on your belly
Just as fast as you can;

And your top shakes a little,
And your bottom shakes a lot,
And your middle gives a twiddle
Till your tummy's in a knot;

Then the jelly starts to wibble
On your jelly-belly-pot—
And you've shake-'n'-baked your jelly,
And you serve it, piping hot!

—Dennis Lee

Runny Egg

For breakfast I had a runny egg.
I chased it round the table.
It wobbled and it screeched at me.
"Catch me if you're able!"

So I nailed it to the table.

—Brian Patten

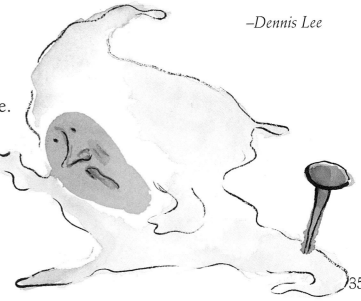

35

Higgledy-Piggledy Takes Out the Garbage

Higgledy-Piggledy
  takes out the garbage.
He whistles and sings
  when he's doing his chores.
He dries all the dishes;
  he washes the windows.

(And I'd like to use him
for mopping up floors!)

–Myra Cohn Livingston

My Mother

My mother was born in England,
My father was born in France,
And me? I was born in diapers
Because I had no pants.

–Anonymous

My Brother's Bug

My brother's bug was green and plump,
it did not run, it could not jump,
it had no fur for it to shed,
it slept all night beneath his bed.

My brother's bug had dainty feet,
it did not need a lot to eat,
it did not need a lot to drink,
it did not scream, it did not stink.

It always tried to be polite,
it did not scratch, it did not bite,
the only time it soiled the rug
was when I squashed my brother's bug.

–Jack Prelutsky

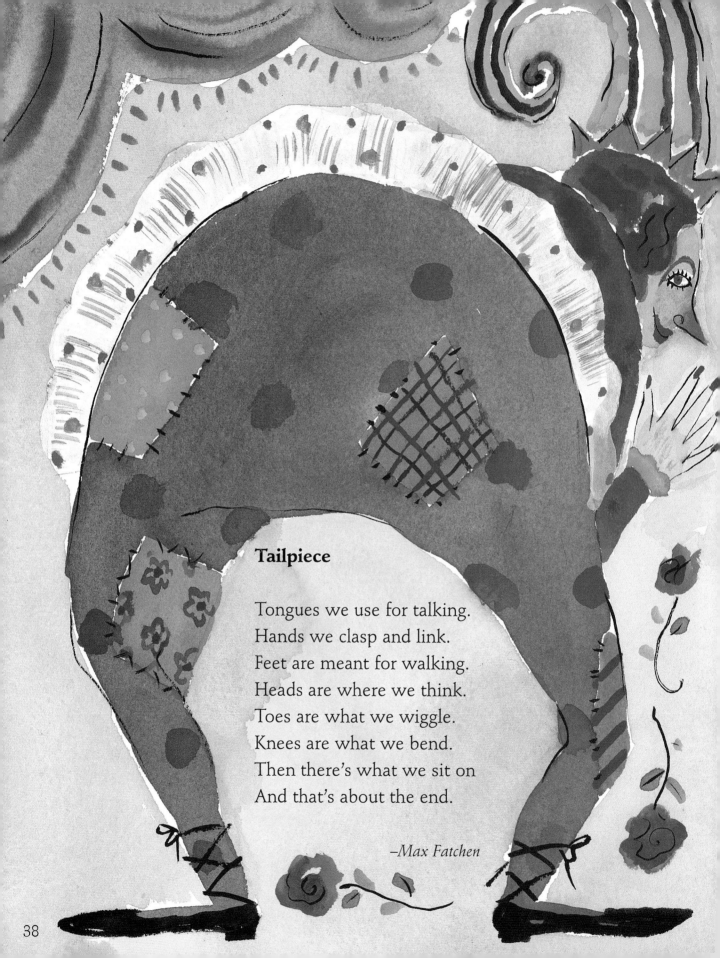

Tailpiece

Tongues we use for talking.
Hands we clasp and link.
Feet are meant for walking.
Heads are where we think.
Toes are what we wiggle.
Knees are what we bend.
Then there's what we sit on
And that's about the end.

–Max Fatchen

TITLE INDEX

AUTHOR INDEX

Acknowledgments

Grateful acknowledgment is made to the following for permission to reprint previously published material:

Bantam Doubleday Dell Publishing Group, Inc., for "Big Bert," from *The Word Party* by Richard Edwards. Copyright © 1986 by Richard Edwards. Used by permission of Delacorte Press, a division of Bantam Doubleday Dell Publishing Group, Inc. "Hi, How Are You Today?," from *The Butterfly Jar* by Jeff Moss. Copyright © 1989 by Jeff Moss. Used by permission of Bantam Books, a division of Bantam Doubleday Dell Publishing Group, Inc.

Boyds Mills Press for "Show and Tell" by David L. Harrison, from Boyds Mills Press, © 1993. "Elephant Rules" and "The Trouble with My House" by David L. Harrison, from *The Boy Who Counted Stars*, by Boyds Mills Press, © 1994. "A Stripeless Tiger" by Arnold Spilka from *Monkeys Write Terrible Letters*, by Boyds Mills Press, © 1994. "Birdseed" and "Gorilla" by Brod Bagert from *Let Me Be the Boss*, by Boyds Mills Press, © 1993. "Contagious" by Brod Bagert from *Chicken Socks*, by Boyds Mills Press, © 1993. "Toes in My Nose" by Sheree Fitch, from *Toes in My Nose*, by Boyds Mills Press, © 1993.

Felicity Bryan for "Groan!" and "Oh, Ozzie!" from *The House That Caught a Cold*. Text copyright © 1991 by Richard Edwards.

Farrar, Straus & Giroux, Inc., for "A Young Lady Named Rose" from *Laughing Time* by William Jay Smith. Copyright © 1990 by William Jay Smith. Reprinted by permission of Farrar, Straus & Giroux, Inc.

Harcourt Brace & Company for "The Hippopotanoose" from *Animal Fare*. Copyright © 1994 by Jane Yolen. Reprinted by permission of Harcourt Brace & Company.

HarperCollins Publishers for "Hula Eel" from *A Light in the Attic*, by Shel Silverstein. Copyright © 1981 by Evil Eye Music, Inc. Selection reprinted by permission of HarperCollins Publishers. "Homemade Boat" from *Where the Sidewalk Ends* by Shel Silverstein. Copyright © 1974 by Evil Eye Music, Inc. Selection reprinted by permission of HarperCollins Publishers. "Noisome Naomi" from *Alpha Beta Chowder* by Jeanne Steig. Copyright © 1992 by Jeanne Steig. "Tell Me I'm Pretty, the Bunny Said" from *Silly Songs and Sad* by Ellen Raskin. Copyright © 1967 by Ellen Raskin. Selection reprinted by permission of HarperCollins Publishers.

HarperCollins Publishers Australia for "A Close-Knit Family" and "Shock Sock" from *Don't Throw Rocks at Chicken Pox* by Bill Condon. Reprinted by permission of HarperCollins Publishers Australia.

HarperCollins Publishers Ltd. for "Shake-'n'-Bake a Jelly" and "Down in Patagonia" by Dennis Lee. Copyright © 1991 by Dennis Lee. From *The Ice Cream Store* by Dennis Lee. Published in Canada by HarperCollins Publishers Ltd. and in the United States by Scholastic, Inc.

Henry Holt & Co., Inc., for "The Crocodile" from *Creatures Great and Small* by Michael Flanders. Copyright © 1964 by Michael Flanders. Reprinted by permission of Henry Holt & Co., Inc.

Houghton Mifflin Co. for "There Seems to Be a Problem" from *The Hopeful Trout and Other Limericks* by John Ciardi. Copyright © 1989 by Myra J. Ciardi. "It Makes No Difference to Me" from *Doodle Soup* by John Ciardi. Copyright © 1985 by Myra J. Ciardi. "Betty Bopper" from *Mummy Took Cooking Lessons* by John Ciardi. Copyright © 1990 by Judith C. Ciardi. All reprinted by permission of Houghton Mifflin Co. All rights reserved.

John Johnson Ltd. for "Tailpiece" and "Hullo, Inside" by Max Fatchen. From *Wry Rhymes for Troublesome Times*. Published by Viking Kestrel and Puffin Books. Copyright © 1983 by Max Fatchen.

Pike Johnson, Jr., for "Ptarmigans" from *Pike's Poems*, copyright © 1992. Reprinted by permission of Pike Johnson, Jr.

Edite Kroll Literary Agency for "New Bicycle" from *Goosebumps & Butterflies* by Yolanda Nave. Copyright © 1990 by Yolanda Nave. By permission of Edite Kroll Literary Agency.

Little, Brown and Company for "The Eel" from *Verses from 1929 On* by Odgen Nash. Copyright 1942 by Ogden Nash. First appeared in *The New Yorker*. By permission of Little, Brown and Company. "Brain Drain" from *The Country Mail Is Coming* by Max Fatchen. Copyright © 1990 by Max Fatchen. By permission of Little, Brown and Company.

Lutterworth Press for "Big Bert" from *The Word Party* by Richard Edwards. Copyright © 1986 by Richard Edwards. Canadian rights granted by permission of Lutterworth Press.

Gina Maccoby Literary Agency for "Hippopotamus" by Mary Ann Hoberman, from *Yellow Butter Purple Jelly Red Jam Black Bread*. Reprinted by permission of Gina Maccoby Literary Agency. Copyright © 1981 by Mary Ann Hoberman.

William Morrow & Company, Inc., for "Sir Samuel Squinn" from *Grim and Ghastly Goings-On* by Florence Parry Heide. Copyright © 1992 by Florence Parry Heide. By permission of Lothrop, Lee & Shepard, a division of William Morrow & Company, Inc. "Although He Didn't Like the Taste" from *Whisker & Rhymes* by Arnold Lobel. Copyright © 1985 by Arnold Lobel. By permission of Greenwillow Books, a division of William Morrow & Company, Inc. "My Brother's Bug" and "We're Fearless Flying Hotdogs" from *Something Big Has Been Here* by Jack Prelutsky, copyright © 1990. "Dragonbrag" from *The Dragons Are Singing Tonight* by Jack Prelutsky, copyright © 1993. By permission of Greenwillow Books, a division of William Morrow & Company, Inc.

Orion Publishing Group for "My Sister" from *Nonstop Nonsense* by Margaret Mahy. Canadian rights granted by permission of Dent Children's Books, a division of Orion Publishing Group.

Penguin Books Ltd. for "Bad Report—Good Manners" from *Unspun Socks from a Chicken's Laundry* by Spike Milligan (Michael Joseph, 1981). Copyright © 1981 by Spike Milligan Productions. Reproduced by permission of Michael Joseph Ltd. "Groan!" and "Oh, Ozzie!" from *The House That Caught a Cold*, by Richard Edwards (Viking Books) 1991. Copyright © 1991 by Richard Edwards. Reproduced by permission of Penguin Books Ltd. (Canadian rights).

Penguin, USA, Inc., for "A Hippopotamusn't" and "Tom Tigercat" from *A Hippopotamusn't* by J. Patrick Lewis. Copyright © 1990 by J. Patrick Lewis. Used by permission of Dial Books for Young Readers, a division of Penguin Books USA, Inc.

Louis Phillips for "The Elephant" from *Oh, Such Foolishness!* by Louis Phillips. Reprinted by permission of the author.

G. P. Putnam's Sons for "The Fossilot" by Jane Yolen. Reprinted by permission of G. P. Putnam's Sons from *Best Witches* by Jane Yolen. Copyright © 1989 by Jane Yolen.

Red Deer College Press for "Skeletons in Restaurants" and "Oh, How Strange." Copyright © 1992 by Paul Duggan. From *Murphy the Rat*, a Northern Lights Children's Book from Red Deer College Press. Reprinted by permission of the publisher.

Marian Reiner Literary Agency for "Harriet, by Magic Force" from *You Be Good & I'll Be Night* by Eve Merriam (Morrow Jr. Books). Copyright © 1988 by Eve Merriam. "Joker" from *Chortles* by Eve Merriam (Morrow Jr. Books). Copyright © 1962, 1964, 1973, 1976, 1989 by Eve Merriam. "The Nose Knows" from *A Poem for a Pickle* by Eve Merriam (Morrow Jr. Books). Copyright © 1989 by Eve Merriam. All are reprinted by permission of Marian Reiner. "I Left My Head" from *See My Lovely Poison Ivy* by Lilian Moore. Copyright © 1975 by Lilian Moore. Reprinted by permission of Marian Reiner for the author.

Rogers, Coleridge & White Ltd. for "Runny Egg" from *Thawing Frozen Frogs* by Brian Patten. Reprinted by permission of Rogers, Coleridge & White Ltd.

Simon & Schuster for "In Her Lunchbox." Reprinted with permission of Margaret K. McElderry Books, an imprint of Simon & Schuster Children's Publishing Division, from *Fresh Brats* by X. J. Kennedy. Copyright © 1990 by X. J. Kennedy. "On a Factory Tour," reprinted with permission of Margaret K. McElderry Books, an imprint of Simon & Schuster Children's Publishing Division, from *Drat These Brats* by X. J. Kennedy. Copyright © 1993 by X. J. Kennedy. "The Vacuum Cleaner's Swallowed Will," reprinted with permission of Margaret K. McElderry Books, an imprint of Simon & Schuster Children's Publishing Division, from *Ghastlies, Goops & Pincushions* by X. J. Kennedy. Copyright © 1989 by X. J. Kennedy. "My Sister," reprinted with permission of Margaret K. McElderry Books, an imprint of Simon & Schuster Children's Publishing Division, from *Nonstop Nonsense* by Margaret Mahy. Copyright © 1977 by Margaret Mahy (USA rights only). "For Neatness and Comfort," reprinted with permission of Margaret K. McElderry Books, an imprint of Simon & Schuster Children's Publishing Division, from *Hurry, Hurry, Mary Dear! and Other Nonsense Poems* by N. M. Bodecker. Copyright © 1976 by N. M. Bodecker. "Higgledy-Piggledy Takes Out the Garbage," reprinted with permission of Margaret K. McElderry Books, an imprint of Simon & Schuster Children's Publishing Division, from *Higgledy-Piggledy* by Myra Cohn Livingston. Copyright © 1986 by Myra Cohn Livingston.

Charles E. Tuttle Co., Inc., for "Wake Up Early" from *A Child's Garden of Weirdness* by Dick Gautier. Copyright © 1993 by Charles E. Tuttle Co., Inc., Boston/Tokyo. Used by permission of Charles E. Tuttle Co., Inc. All rights reserved.

Walker Books Ltd. for "The Crocodile's Dentist" from *Moonfrog*. Copyright © 1992 by Richard Edwards. Published in the USA by Candlewick Press, permission granted by Walker Books Ltd. "Ancient Egyptian Joke" from *Making Friends with Frankenstein*. Copyright © 1993 by Colin McNaughton. Published in the USA by Candlewick Press. Permission granted by Walker Books Ltd. "Bomb Appetit!" and "The Human Beanpole" from *Who's Been Sleeping in My Porridge?* Copyright © 1990 by Colin McNaughton. Published in the UK by Walker Books Ltd.

Colin West for "Pangolin" from *The Best of the West* by Colin West. Copyright © 1990 by Colin West. Reprinted by permission of the author. "Insides" from *What Would You Do with a Wobble-Dee-Woo?* Copyright © 1988 by Colin West. Reprinted by permission of the author.